BreakThrough

discovering the compassion and power of Jesus

A seven-week adventure in the Gospel of Mark

By Vicki & Jim Egli

ampelon
publishing

BreakThrough
Copyright ©2005 by Vicki & Jim Egli

ISBN: 0-9748825-4-2

Printed in the United States of America

Requests for information should be addressed to:
Ampelon Publishing
6920 Jimmy Carter Blvd., Ste. 200
Norcross, GA 30071

To order other Ampelon Publishing products, visit us on the web at: www.ampelonpublishing.com

Visit Vineyard Champaign on the web at:
www.vineyardchampaign.org

Table of
Contents

BreakThrough

BreakThrough

Mark's Gospel

The Gospel of Mark tells a fast-paced story. It succinctly but powerfully presents the good news of Jesus. Early Christian historians tell us that Mark wrote his gospel based on the Apostle Peter's firsthand accounts. This is most likely true. Mark includes vivid details that the other gospel writers left out, and the details are especially rich in the stories that directly involve Peter.

This gospel is all about breakthrough. It describes the awesome news of the arrival of God's Kingdom. It announces that in Jesus, God's power, compassion, forgiveness, and freedom have invaded our world. As you encounter Jesus over your daily readings in the weeks ahead, you will see that many people received breakthroughs from Jesus. The sick were healed, the guilty were forgiven, the outcasts were accepted, the demonized were set free!

Those that wanted Jesus' touch in the gospel of Mark got it. But they often had to push through. The four men bringing their paralyzed friend couldn't pass through the crowd to get to Jesus, so they dug a hole in the roof. A woman in need of healing pushed through a jostling crowd to touch the hem of Jesus' robe. A blind man named Bartimaeus cried out for Jesus' help even though everyone around him was telling him to shut up.

As you read Mark's story, allow yourself to enter into it. Who do you identify with in each episode? How would you have reacted to Jesus if you had been there yourself? What do you see Jesus doing? What do you want him to do in your life? What is he asking of his listeners? What is he asking of you right now?

BreakThrough

Getting the Most out of Your Time

F irst of all, set aside a time each day for God. Choose a time when you are least likely to be interrupted. You may find that you can get through the material in 10 minutes, but if you want to get more from the study, plan to spend 20 or 30 minutes a day.

This book offers seven weeks of devotions. Each week has an introduction and five daily devotionals. You can spend one day reading the introduction and skimming through the week's readings to prepare you for the upcoming days. Five days a week you will read a section of the gospel of Mark. A short summary and some questions designed to help you see how this passage applies to your past, present, and future follow the scripture reading. If you take time each day to answer these questions thoughtfully, you will have a wonderful record of God's activity in your life up to the present as well as faith in your heart for what God wants to do in you today and in your future.

These daily meditations are meant to draw you into Mark's gospel so that you might encounter Jesus himself. Over the next seven weeks, we invite you to experience him in a profound and life-changing way.

Week One Introduction

Mark 1:15
*"The Kingdom of God is near! Turn from your sins and
believe this good news."*

J esus launched his ministry with the dramatic declaration, "At
last the time has come! The Kingdom of God is near! Turn
from your sins and believe this Good News!" (Mark 1:15).
Through his words and his actions Jesus announced that God's
long awaited Kingdom was crashing into the present (Luke 11:20;
17:20-21).

What is "the Kingdom of God"? It is God's rule or reign
with all its incredible benefits—eternal life, wholeness, hope,
prosperity, love, and forgiveness. The apostle Paul succinctly
defined the Kingdom as "righteousness, peace, and joy in the
Holy Spirit" (Romans 14:17, NIV).

New Testament scholar George Eldon Ladd, in his book *The
Gospel of the Kingdom,* helpfully explained Jesus' Kingdom
declaration. In Jesus' time, the Jews were expecting God to break
into their world and usher in a new age. Their view of history
could be illustrated with this simple timeline:

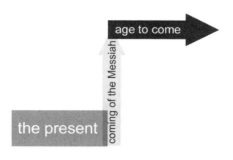

Jesus, however, taught and demonstrated a different perspective. In the New Testament, we see a view of history that can be illustrated like this:

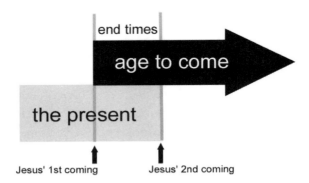

Jesus came proclaiming and offering the benefits of God's Kingdom—his salvation, wholeness, deliverance, and healing. However, God's Kingdom is not yet present in its fullness. We live in-between, in the time of the already-but-not-yet, in the overlap of this age and the age to come.

But the good news is that even now we can enter into God's Kingdom. We can have a new relationship with God through Jesus. We can already experience the life of the age to come, in the midst of the challenges of this current age. In response to this amazing good news, Jesus invites us: "Turn from your sins and believe this Good News!"

In the gospel of Mark, people responded to Jesus in many different ways. Many reached out for his offer of forgiveness, love, healing, and freedom. Some surrendered to him. Others turned away. How will you respond to Jesus' invitation today?

BreakThrough

Jesus Has Good News to Share

Read: Mark 1:1-20

J esus calls us to a great adventure. He offers us the good news of God's Kingdom, inviting us to turn from our sins, leave behind distractions, and learn from him.

John the Baptist came before Jesus, challenging people to turn to God to be forgiven. He baptized people when they were willing to confess their need for God. But he made it clear that someone was coming after him who could do more than forgive sins—he could baptize with the Holy Spirit!

As we study the book of Mark together, let's find out all we can about Jesus. Who is this person who is God's beloved Son? What does it mean that he will baptize us with the Holy Spirit? And what did Jesus mean when he announced that the Kingdom of God is near? What made Jesus so appealing, that men would leave the lives they knew to follow him?

Look Back

Jesus called Simon, Andrew, James, and John to be his disciples. They chose to leave behind their family businesses to follow him. When did you first hear Jesus calling you to be his disciple?

What emotions did you experience, or what thoughts did you have?

BreakThrough

How easy of a decision was it for you to follow Christ? (Or are you still considering his claims?)

What has it cost you?

How has your decision been worthwhile?

Look Forward

Jesus continually invites us to follow him. He calls to you today — "Come, be my disciple, and I will show you how to fish for people."

How will you respond to that call today?

Jesus Comes with Authority

Read: Mark 1:21-39

After Jesus taught in the synagogue, people were amazed at his authority, and immediately the power of Satan's Kingdom and God's Kingdom clashed. Jesus demonstrated the authority of God's rule by freeing a man from an evil spirit. News about him spread quickly. By evening, crowds of people came to Jesus, hoping to be healed or at least to watch the action. They were not disappointed. Great numbers were healed; many demons were cast out. The next morning they came back for more.

But where was Jesus? Everyone was asking for him! His disciples frantically searched for him, finally finding him alone in the wilderness praying. He told them it was time to leave the crowds behind and move on.

Jesus had a heart to obey God. He wasn't free to do whatever he wanted; he was under authority. And as he slipped away in the early morning to pray, he gained the wisdom and courage to leave a successful healing ministry in the comfort of Capernaum, the city where he lived, in order to obey his Father. He knew what he needed to do: travel from town to town, preaching and expelling demons — declaring and demonstrating God's Kingdom, the presence of the future invading our world.

Look Back

Jesus had authority from God to teach, heal, and cast out demons. He unselfishly gave his life to that ministry. But he did not allow others to set his agenda: he took time to hear from God,

BreakThrough

then boldly did whatever the Father gave him to do.

When you have taken time to hear from God recently, what message do you feel like he is conveying?

When have you been amazed at the authority Jesus has demonstrated in your life?

Look Forward

As Jesus' follower, you are empowered and called to speak his words and do his works. He has amazing things he wants to do through you and has given you his authority to do them.

When will you spend time talking to God today?

How do you think he specifically wants to use you today? (Ask him if you're not sure.)

Ask God for the power and courage to obey, and record how he uses you!

Being Generous with God's love forgiveness & Acceptance

BreakThrough

Who Receives the Kingdom?

Read: Mark 1:40-2:17

Jesus makes it clear that he wants to help anyone who wants help (Mark 1:41, 2:17). And beyond that, he actually can and does help them! While others stayed away from people with leprosy, Jesus compassionately touched and healed them. He forgave and healed the paralytic and joined in a party with the "scum" of the city. People from everywhere were praising God for the amazing ways Jesus reached out and helped others.

But not everyone responded with praise. The Pharisees thought that Jesus was being much too *Being* generous with God's *love* forgiveness and acceptance. They thought that God only loved and welcomed the most religious people and were more concerned about rules and regulations than about people's hurts and struggles. They expected a different type of Messiah and a different kind of Kingdom.

Look Back

Jesus reached out to those who needed help—to misfits. How have you seen Jesus do this in your own life?

How do you relate to these stories: Were you a misfit Jesus helped? Has he asked you to reach out to misfits in the past? Or have you been more like the Pharisees, uncomfortable relating to those who don't quite have it all together?

BreakThrough

Were you able to reach out to someone in response to yesterday's "Look Forward?" Write about what happened.

Look Forward

Jesus is still healing, forgiving, and offering belonging. What needs do you want to bring to him today (Either your own needs or those of someone close to you)?

List any bad attitudes toward others from which you might need to repent. Ask Jesus to use you again today to touch others with his love.

What opportunities will you have to reach out to someone today?

BreakThrough

Jesus Wants Us to Enjoy Life!

Read: Mark 2:18-3:6

I t's time to celebrate! When people wondered why Jesus'
disciples didn't fast, Jesus told the bewildered people that they
couldn't fast at a wedding party! He wanted them to know that
he was bringing a whole new way of life, and things would never
be the same again. He wasn't just trying to patch up what had
gone bad; he was starting all over! In Jesus, the presence of the
future has come – it's party time!

In the stories of eating grain and healing on the Sabbath, Jesus
showed that God's laws were meant for our benefit, not to be
used as fences to determine who was in and who was out. God
loves us, and he created the Sabbath for our health.

But again we see that the Pharisees just couldn't handle the
fact that Jesus was greater than the religious system they were trying so desperately to control. They started making plans to destroy
Jesus.

Look Back

When have you wanted to celebrate because Jesus did
something wonderful for you?

BreakThrough

Look Forward

In the Old Testament, people sometimes fasted when they were experiencing difficult times. Jesus indicates that there will be times of fasting for us as well as times of celebration. Which time are you experiencing right now and how has it impacted your life?

Write a prayer telling God about the situation you find yourself in today, whether it's something to celebrate or something to fast about. Thank God that he is with you in the hard times as well as the fun times.

What Is Jesus Really up to?

Read: Mark 3:7-3:35

T ry to imagine the crowd of people gathering to get close enough to see everything Jesus was doing—something like a big mosh pit at a concert, anxious to get in on the action. How exciting to see the healings and the shrieking demons! But Jesus wasn't content just to put on a show. He took time to choose twelve friends to be his close companions and with whom to share his lifestyle. He gave them his authority to preach and cast out demons.

While some people were thrilled by what Jesus was doing, others were totally opposed to him. His family thought he was crazy and came to take him away. The religious leaders claimed he must be possessed by Satan. But in the midst of opposition, Jesus pointed out that he was overcoming Satan by God's Spirit and that God was pulling together a new family built on doing His will.

Look Back

What drew you to Jesus?

Was there ever a time when you felt Jesus call you out of the crowd to be his companion and share his lifestyle? What was this experience like for you?

BreakThrough

Look Forward

Jesus continues to overcome Satan by the power of God's Spirit. What is your response to the Holy Spirit?

Write down some areas of your life that need to come more completely under God's reign. Ask God to give you the strength to relinquish control of them.

God is still creating a new family. Ask for a deeper sense of belonging to God's loving family. Pray for a heart to actively include others in that wonderful family.

Write down the names of anyone you feel God is asking you to get closer to.

BreakThrough

Week Two Introduction

Mark 4:25
*"To those who are open to my teaching, more understanding
will be given. But to those who are not listening, even what
they have will be taken away from them."*

What is the Kingdom of God? How does it work? Why does Kingdom breakthrough often start in small, almost imperceptible ways? In our next section of Mark's gospel, Jesus began telling simple stories – parables to help us understand the mysteries of God's Kingdom.

One thing is clear in what Jesus taught and did: God's Kingdom offers abundance. Although some may reject the good news and others accept it on only a superficial level, those who truly take it to heart will "produce a huge harvest—thirty, sixty, or even a hundred times as much as had been planted" (Mark 4:20). God's Kingdom offers power to go beyond the possible to the impossible. As you will see, the man hopelessly demonized was set free. The disciples caught in a storm were delivered. The woman beyond the help of doctors was healed. Even the dead were raised to life!

What hopeless situation are you facing? What situation do you see in your own life or the life of a loved one that looks impossible? In Jesus, the impossible becomes possible as the power of God's Kingdom infiltrates our world.

As you read this week, notice how people responded to God's power released in Jesus. Some reached out for it. Some were offended. The disciples were often both amazed and perplexed.

BreakThrough ... of fruitfulness and freedom

Just when it looks like things cannot get any more incredible, Jesus takes things to a whole new level by multiplying his ministry through others. The authority he had been demonstrating he passed on to his followers, sending them out to do his works and share his words. Mark tells us, "So the disciples went out, telling all they met to turn from their sins. And they cast out many demons and healed many sick people, anointing them with olive oil" (Mark 6:12-13).

God's Kingdom can bring incredible freedom and fruitfulness in your life. Jesus wants to do amazing, impossible things in you and through you! Do you want to receive? Do you want to be used? If so, listen up! Jesus tells you, "Anyone who is willing to hear should listen and understand! And be sure to pay attention to what you hear. The more you do this, the more you will understand—and even more, besides. To those who are open to my teaching, more understanding will be given. But to those who are not listening, even what they have will be taken away from them" (Mark 4:23-25). Pay attention. Stay tuned. Let's embrace all that Jesus is saying to us and doing among us.

BreakThrough

Jesus Offers Fruitfulness

Read: Mark 4:1-20

In this chapter, Mark tells us some of the stories or parables that Jesus used in his teaching. They were almost like riddles. People could enjoy each story as Jesus told it, but they could only guess at its meaning. Those who wanted to know what the stories meant would have to ask him. Those who were not willing to come to Jesus would never understand and could never be forgiven apart from him. He alone brought understanding about the mystery of the Kingdom of God.

In this story Jesus assured us that God wants his message to reach everyone. How people respond to God's message makes all the difference. Some don't let it affect them at all. Some think it sounds good until they realize the consequences. Others believe it's true but choose to live for themselves instead. Thankfully, some allow it to penetrate their lives and change the way they live, producing wonderful results. God's Kingdom is breaking through; what we receive is up to us. How will you respond?

Look Back

What have been the hardest things for you to understand about God? How have you tried to get answers?

BreakThrough

Describe a moment when something you were struggling to understand about God came to light for you.

Look Forward

Jesus wonders if we can't understand this story how we could understand any of the rest of his stories. This story isn't primarily about us though; it's about the amazing power of God—the presence of God's Kingdom breaking into our lives. Our part is simply to receive God's message, allowing him to teach us "the secret about the Kingdom of God" (see verses 11-13). If we do, God will do amazing things in and through our lives. Jesus wants us to experience abundant life that produces wonderful results.

Write down any obstacles you sense are keeping you from letting God's message penetrate your life and change the way you live.

Pray and ask God to give you eyes to see, ears to hear, and a heart that is willing to turn from sin and be forgiven. Ask him to teach you about the secrets of the Kingdom of God and let him produce amazing fruitfulness!

Jesus Describes the Kingdom of God

Read: Mark 4:21-34

Remember from yesterday that Jesus said it was important to understand the parable of the farmer planting his seed in order to understand his other parables? The Kingdom will produce a huge harvest when someone receives it! In today's parables, he continued to teach about the amazing nature of the Kingdom of God. The emphasis was not on what people do, but on what happens when they believe his message and act on it.

First, we see that the Kingdom isn't something to keep hidden. No, we bring it out and shine it all around so that its wonderful light exposes the darkness and helps us see and understand. Jesus also encourages us not to despise small beginnings. Our initial Kingdom breakthroughs might seem small, like tiny mustard seeds. But once the Kingdom has taken root in our lives, it just keeps on growing, producing big results.

Jesus wasn't primarily talking about what happens in each individual's life, though we can apply his truth personally. His teaching implies that if we as members of his Kingdom are shining his light and letting him teach us his ways, we will have a tremendous impact on the society in which we live. We will be a community of hope in a lost and despairing world.

Look Back

Throughout history, the organized church has often failed to shine the light of Christ, but the gospel of Jesus has had incredible influence on societies nevertheless. Consider the abolition of slavery in Great Britain or the saving of unborn children's lives

BreakThrough

through Crisis Pregnancy Centers. God's Kingdom has broken into this world in many powerful ways since Jesus came proclaiming it.

Whom has God used to shine his light on you? How did God use you to impact their lives?

Write a prayer thanking God for the impact that his gospel has had on your life.

Look Forward

In what ways does Jesus want to shine his light through you? (Whose life does he want to light up through you?)

Many candles produce much more light than one candle by itself. Whom is God calling you to partner with so that your life can have a growing impact on others?

BreakThrough

Week Two
Day Three

Jesus Offers Freedom from Fear

Read: Mark 4:35-5:20

Jesus was ready to leave. As he and his disciples crossed the lake in the little fishing boat he had been teaching from, he fell asleep. The disciples panicked when a storm came up. Then Jesus' response to their cry for help put more fear into them than the storm itself! The disciples didn't yet understand who Jesus was. How could anyone stop a storm?

Reaching the other side of the lake, they were confronted by a man oppressed by evil spirits. God's Kingdom again clashed with the powers of Satan. Jesus took authority over the spirits and cast them into a herd of pigs that consequently went crashing into the lake. Fear gripped the crowd that gathered, and they begged Jesus to leave.

Only the man who had been freed wasn't afraid. In fact, he wanted to go with Jesus. When Jesus asked him to stay and tell his friends what had happened, the man told everyone he could about the great things Jesus had done for him. Whether it is personal problems or relationship problems, Jesus can set us free from situations that cause us great anxiety.

Look Back

Jesus took authority over nature and over evil spirits in order to bring freedom for those who were oppressed. The results were drastic and overwhelming and could not be overlooked. How have you reacted to Jesus' miracles?

BreakThrough

Look Forward

Write down some circumstances in your life or in the life of someone you care about that need a miraculous intervention from Jesus.

Write a prayer, inviting God's Kingdom to break through!

BreakThrough

Jesus Has Good News to Share

Read: Mark 5:21-6:6

After appearing to hit homeruns along the shores of Lake Galilee—freeing the demonized, healing the sick, raising the dead—it looked like Jesus struck out in his hometown of Nazareth. People there limited what Jesus could do because they were looking at who he was in a natural sense, not who the Holy Spirit was enabling him to be. "God can't work through someone as ordinary as a builder's son," they thought. Remember that God chose to send his Son as a very ordinary person from an ordinary family with ordinary problems. He really looked like no one special. Yet through his obedience, God used him to be the savior of the world. Fulfilling his ultimate mission depended on his own response to God's voice, not the response of others. Of course, none of us will be the savior of the world. But we each can fulfill the unique call of God on our lives whether or not those around us have the faith to see it.

In Nazareth, the lack of miracles was from lack of faith. But the point of the story isn't to say that when we don't see healing it's always because of lack of faith. We can't make that assumption. Because we live in the "already-but-not-yet," we will often see God heal, but sometimes we won't. We should just keep asking, keep praying, keep risking, and keep expecting because we want to be there when the Kingdom breaks through. We want to be alongside Jairus and the woman who touched Jesus' robe, not with the hometown crowd from Nazareth.

BreakThrough

Look Back

Take an honest look at your attitude toward healing before God. Do you identify more with Jairus, the woman, the crowd at Nazareth, or onlookers? Are you part of the crowd who is watching Jesus, just waiting to see what he'll do next? Or are you part of the crowd that's laughing and scoffing that Jesus can't possibly fix the problem at hand?

Look Forward

Jesus still heals. It's those who believe who get to see. To those who have, even more is given. Sometimes we experience dramatic healing; sometimes there seem to be barriers that prevent it. Ask God to let you be a part of his healing ministry, and then take the opportunities he gives you. Take risks. Ask God to break through; his rule is here! If you're already involved in praying for healing, invite others to pray alongside you so they can witness a miracle first hand! Record one of your stories here and share it to build the faith of others.

Write down what you think God is calling you to do as a next step in partnering with him in healing others.

Jesus Shares His Authority

Read: Mark 6:6-6:29

When Jesus called his first disciples, he promised them that he would make them fishers of men. He had modeled for them how to teach, heal, and cast out demons. Then he expected them to be able to do the same, because he gave them his authority. That was how he equipped them to extend his ministry to the other towns in the area. He warned them that they wouldn't always be warmly received, and told them not to waste their time in unreceptive places. Many people were healed and delivered through their ministry.

Jesus' growing ministry caught the attention of the local political ruler, Herod Antipas. We get a picture of the political atmosphere and the kind of person Herod was in the account of his party and execution of John the Baptist. Clearly, anyone who was a threat to the established system faced threat of extermination.

Look Back

Jesus asked his disciples to "travel light." He had a specific task for them to do, and extra baggage was more likely to weigh them down than to come in handy. Jesus has work for you to do too. Has he asked you to get rid of any extra "baggage" you're carrying around? How have you responded?

BreakThrough

Look Forward

Jesus wants to demonstrate his authority through you. He's sending you out just as he sent his disciples out—not alone. Who is he sending you with? (Maybe the same people you wrote down in day 2 this week.)

How have you placed your life fully under his authority?

Is there any more extra baggage that Jesus is asking you to leave behind at this point in your life? Write a prayer, submitting to God and inviting him to empower you afresh with his Spirit to continue the ministry of Jesus.

BreakThrough

Week Three Introduction

Mark 7:37
Again and again they said, "Everything he does is wonderful. He even heals those who are deaf and mute."

J esus was a miracle worker. Over and over again he made the impossible possible. He gave sight to the blind and hearing to the deaf, he cleansed the lepers, multiplied the loaves and fish, calmed stormy seas, and raised the dead. Because of his miracles, people knew that God's Kingdom had come near.

Miracles announce that God is both loving and powerful. If God were loving but weak, we wouldn't see miracles. If God were powerful but didn't care about us, we would not see his wonders in our lives. But because he is both loving and powerful, it's natural to expect his miraculous presence in our everyday lives.

One of the biggest miracles recorded in the Gospel of Mark can easily go unnoticed. It's Jesus' creation of a community of hope. One of the first things Jesus did when he launched his ministry was begin shaping a new community. Immediately after he began preaching, Jesus called Andrew and Simon and James and John to follow him (Mark 1:14-20). Several days later, he challenged Levi to join their group (Mark 2:14). In chapter 3, he signalled the beginning of a new people of God. Just as the nation Israel had twelve tribes, Jesus chose twelve apostles to launch a new people. Their first assignment was simply to "be with him" (Mark 3:14). Later he made it clear that he was shaping a new family as he declared, "Whoever does God's will is my brother and sister and mother" (Mark 3:35).

BreakThrough

In chapter 10, when pragmatic Peter asked Jesus what he and the other disciples would get in exchange for following him, Jesus pointed to the new community when he said, "I assure you that everyone who has given up house or brothers or sisters or mother or father or children or property, for my sake and for the Good News, will receive now in return, a hundred times over, houses, brothers, sisters, mothers, children, and property—with persecutions. And in the world to come they will have eternal life" (Mark 10:29-30).

This new community is a family of grace that welcomes the society's outcasts and embraces the sinners rejected by the religious establishment, all the while calling everyone to a new way of life. Jesus shocked his followers by declaring and demonstrating that it is an upside-down community where greatness comes through service instead of power. He instructed them, "Whoever wants to become great among you must be your servant, and whoever wants to be first must be the slave of all. For even the Son of Man did not come to be served, but to serve, and to give his life as a ransom for many" (Mark 10:43-45).

In our fractured world of broken families, strained relationships, and warring nations, one of God's greatest miracles— then as now—is a community of hope that extends God's mercy. In this present age God's family won't be perfect, but we can still be Jesus' people of healing and hope. God can demonstrate his gracious Kingdom through us to a world searching for compassion and belonging.

This week, consider: Where do you need God's miraculous intervention? Who do you know that needs healing, hope, deliverance, or belonging?

BreakThrough

Jesus Shows Compassion through the Miraculous

Read: Mark 6:30-44

Jesus was not controlled by people, but he cared about them. When he saw that his disciples needed a break after their ministry tour, he took them away so they could rest. When the crowd caught up with them, he had compassion on the crowd because "they were like sheep without a shepherd" (Mark 6:34).

People in Israel were looking for a Messiah to lead them to freedom from the oppressive foreign government. Perhaps these 5,000 men had gathered in this remote spot to see if Jesus would launch a military revolt. Maybe they had come to see more miracles. In any case, Jesus' compassion for them stirred him to teach them and then feed them.

Jesus blessed the bread and fish and broke them into pieces so others could eat. Soon his body would be the bread broken for them. Just as God had provided manna in the wilderness, God provided bread for this gathering in the wilderness. Just as God used Moses to lead his people out of an oppressive situation, so God was using Jesus to free his people. But this time he was not setting up another earthly government; he was ushering in the Kingdom of God. In the age to come there will be no hunger; in this miracle that future age was breaking through!

Look Back

How has God provided for your physical needs through the years? Write a prayer of thanks for what God has provided for you. Be specific!

BreakThrough

Look Forward

Jesus wants us to have his compassion for others when they are in need (see James 2:14-17 and 1 John 3:16-17). Sometimes we can help with the resources we have, but sometimes we come up against something like feeding 5,000 with a sack lunch. Then it's time for a miracle. Who do you know that has limited resources and needs your help?

What small (or large) thing is God asking you to offer to help in that situation?

What kind of a miracle would you like to see Jesus do? Ask God to release breakthroughs of his mercy and provision to you and others.

When Jesus Prays, Things Happen

Read: Mark 6:45-56

Jesus made time to pray. He sent the crowd and his disciples away in two different directions and went off by himself to have some time alone with God and focus his life. After he had prayed, he was ready to cross the lake himself. By now the disciples were in the middle of the lake battling a strong head wind. In the midst of their struggle, Jesus came walking past them on the water. They didn't recognize him. They were terrified. Even after he had calmed the wind and joined them in the boat, they really didn't know what to think.

Maybe they were experiencing "miracle overload." They'd just seen demons cast out and people healed as they went from town to town, a crowd of 5,000 miraculously fed, and Jesus walk on water and calm a storm. They probably couldn't remember the last time they'd slept in their own beds. When they reached shore the next morning, they still couldn't get the rest they needed because anyone who recognized Jesus ran and got sick friends and relatives for him to heal. When would they ever get a break?

Look Back

Jesus kept his calm through spending time with his Father. When in your life have you had a close relationship with God?

What helps you set time aside to be with him?

BreakThrough

What helps you feel close to God?

Look Forward

Jesus is unpredictable. The only way to be prepared for what he'll do next is to keep taking time with him, just like he took time to pray in this story. How are you cultivating a deeper relationship with Jesus?

Write down your plan to keep taking time with him. (If you need further wisdom or encouragement, talk and pray with a friend or family member about the next steps in your walk with God).

Who Has Sincere Faith?

Read: Mark 7:1-30

Jesus was a Jew, and he says in verse 27 that he came to help his own people, the Jews. But in today's reading we see the continued conflict between Jesus and the Jewish religious leaders. Many of the Jewish religious leaders were so critical of Jesus' approach to life that they refused to listen to him. They were concerned about outward traditions that confirmed their identity as Jews, rather than the condition of their hearts.

In contrast, the Gentile woman from Tyre had much faith. Although she was not a Jew, she put her faith in Jesus. She realized he could heal her daughter and begged him for help. Jesus made it plain that his mission was to the Jews, but that didn't keep him from healing her daughter when the woman was persistent and begged for help out of her need, out of who Jesus was and not because of who she was.

Look Back

Whom do you identify most with: the woman from Tyre who knew she didn't deserve help but begged Jesus anyway, the religious leaders who wanted to set the rules and make sure everyone else toed the line, or the disciples who were just trying to figure out what was going on? Why?

BreakThrough

Look Forward

John 1:11-12 says, "Even in his own land and among his own people, he was not accepted. But to all who believed him and accepted him, he gave the right to become children of God." Our world has plenty of people like the woman from Tyre who don't fit into the established religious system of the day. But they, like her, need a touch from Jesus. They just need to know he's come to town and is ready to help them. Who in your world might fit that description?

How might you share what Jesus is doing in your life with them, so they'll know "he's in town"?

Write a prayer for them and for yourself as you relate to them.

Break**Through**

Week Three
Day Four

Jesus Ministers in Gentile Territory

Read: Mark 7:31-8:10

Jesus was in an area where the Jews were in the minority. Would he try to keep to himself, or would he help the Gentiles? When a deaf man was brought to him, Jesus healed not only his hearing but also his speech! Isaiah had prophesied to the Israelites many years earlier, "Say to those who are afraid, 'Be strong, and do not fear, for your God is coming to destroy your enemies. He is coming to save you.' And when he comes, he will open the eyes of the blind and unstop the ears of the deaf. The lame will leap like a deer, and those who cannot speak will shout and sing!" (Isaiah 35:4-6). Jesus was fulfilling this prophesy in a largely Gentile area. Another crowd gathered in amazement.

Once again Jesus found himself in the midst of a large crowd with no food. Once again his compassion prompted a miracle that foreshadowed the breaking of his body for others. Only this time the miracle took place in Gentile territory. Likewise, his death would be a death for all people, not just for the Jews.

Look Back

The disciples still seem to be having a hard time expecting the miraculous, even though they had recently seen Jesus feed a crowd of 5,000 in a similar situation. What would it have been like to be one of Jesus' disciples, traveling into foreign territory with him and seeing him work miracles among people you thought of as beyond God's help? Jot down your thoughts.

BreakThrough

How about you? Have you ever seen a miracle? Write down what it was like.

Look Forward

We can expect Jesus to do miracles in this "foreign land!" He has compassion for us and sees our needs. Take a few minutes and ask the Holy Spirit to show you where he wants to break through with the miraculous in your life.

Now write down the miracles you think the Holy Spirit has put on your heart.

Get up some guts and write specific prayers for each of these miracles. Set a date you'd like to see them answered by if that's appropriate. (We'll be coming back to these in the weeks to come). Remember: It's those who ask that receive! (See Luke 11:9-10 and 1 John 5:14-15).

Who Sees the Miraculous?

Read: Mark 8:11-26

Jesus was not willing to give the Pharisees a miraculous sign to prove he was from God. Jesus performed miracles out of compassion and in response to faith. But when asked to perform a miracle "on demand," Jesus sighed deeply, refused, and crossed to the other side of the lake.

While in the boat, Jesus warned his disciples against becoming like the Pharisees—concerned about religious appearances but blind to the wonderful breakthrough of the Kingdom of God that he had already so clearly demonstrated. Unfortunately, his disciples didn't seem much better off. They still were having trouble seeing who Jesus was and what he wanted to do for them.

But there was still hope for them. In Bethsaida a blind man received his sight. He didn't see clearly at first—the healing took some time, but Jesus was persistent. He stayed with the man until he could see everything clearly. When we're physically blind, we know we can't see what others see. But sometimes we're totally unaware of spiritual blindness. The disciples would eventually see, too.

Look Back

Jesus is used to people taking a long time to see him. He trained his disciples for three years! What is one area you've had trouble in, either in understanding God or in changing something in yourself?

BreakThrough

The disciples had a different problem than the Pharisees. The Pharisees were not willing to see; the disciples just couldn't quite get it. Allow God to examine your heart about the issue you wrote above. Have you been unwilling to learn, or has it just been really hard for you? Explain.

Look Forward

If you've been unwilling, ask God for forgiveness. If it's just been difficult, ask for eyes to see God's power and faith to receive his help. Write your prayer here:

Remember: Keep asking God for the miracles you wrote down yesterday!

BreakThrough

Week Four Introduction

Mark 8:35
"If you try to keep your life for yourself, you will lose it. But if you give up your life for my sake and for the sake of the Good News, you will find true life."

A pivotal passage stands at the heart of Mark's Gospel. Up to this point in the story everyone was perplexed, trying to figure out who Jesus is. Even his bewildered disciples were asking, "Who is this man, that even the wind and waves obey him?" (Mark 4:41)

Jesus, by his words and actions, had been declaring the good news of God's Kingdom. At the same time, he avoided using the politically-loaded term *Messiah* (or Christ) to refer to himself. Instead he chose an obscure Old Testament title, "the Son of Man," to talk about himself – a term that he could fill with new meaning, a term with clear biblical connection to the Kingdom of God (Daniel 7:13-14).

Jesus then brought the issue of his identity to a head. First he asked his disciples, "Who do people say I am?" (Mark 8:27) Then he probed directly, "Who do you say I am?" Peter correctly responded, "You are the Christ" (8:29). But soon Peter revealed that he really didn't know what he was talking about. He knew who Jesus was, but he didn't understand his mission. Like the blind man in the preceding story who only saw a blur after his first touch from Jesus, so Peter could only partially comprehend Jesus's identity. A king who will suffer and die for others? Peter tried to set Jesus straight. But Jesus replied, "Peter, get out of my way! Satan, get lost! You have no idea how God works!" (8:33, Msg.).

BreakThrough

Three times Jesus gave the disciples a brain-whack. Three times he patiently explained that he would be betrayed, undergo incredible suffering, and give up his life. Three times they didn't get it – they attempted to correct what he was saying (Mark 8:32), they argued about which of them was greatest (Mark 9:34), and they vied for the top positions (Mark 10:37). In response, three times Jesus outlined the true nature of the Kingdom of God: we can only gain true life by losing our life (Mark 8:34-38), if someone wants to be first he "must be the servant of all" (Mark 9:35), and "whoever wants to be a leader among you must be your servant" (Mark 10:43).

Jesus offers a path to fullness of life. But first we must let go of all that we have. Jesus announced, "If any of you wants to be my follower, you must put aside your selfish ambition, shoulder your cross, and follow me. If you try to keep your life for yourself, you will lose it. But if you give up your life for my sake and for the sake of the Good News, you will find true life" (Mark 8:34-35). This is the paradox of the Kingdom of God.

If we had been there, would we have grasped the nature of this new King and this new Kingdom? Surely not. Do we even comprehend its truth today?

Like You did for the blind man and Peter, Lord, give us a second touch. Open our hearts and our eyes to receive your offer of abundant, eternal life.

BreakThrough

Jesus Offers Real Life

Read: Mark 8:27-9:13

The disciples had finally understood who Jesus was – the Messiah. But now Jesus needed to teach them just what that was going to mean. Jesus knew he had a mission to fulfill, and he knew it would include suffering and lead to death. He also knew that death was not the end. He was confident not only of rising from the dead but returning in the glory of his Father.

To Jesus the presence of the future was very real. He could make his decisions confident of what was before him. He could see past death to the ultimate victory of his Father. He knew that the way to glory was the way of suffering.

Jesus presented a whole new way of life – the life of the future invading the present – a life devoted to obeying God no matter what the cost, a life that didn't consider personal wealth or comfort, but was totally dedicated to living for God and others. He called his listeners to shoulder their cross. They were familiar with the sight of people carrying crosses on their way to crucifixion. A person carrying a cross was going to die. Jesus explained that the way to find real life is to totally   surrender to God.

Look Back

What have you "put aside" in order to follow Jesus? Would you say you live for yourself, or do you live for God?

BreakThrough

Have you found true life? Describe what that is like for you.

Look Forward

The life Jesus offers is so awesome that it cannot even be compared to life apart from him. Jesus invites us to experience true life by giving up our life for him. Jesus will help you give up anything that's keeping you from true life if you confess it to him.

What are the things keeping you back from totally living for him?

Write a prayer from your heart expressing your desire for true life.

BreakThrough

Jesus Delivers

Read: Mark 9:14-32

J esus had given his disciples Kingdom authority to cast out evil spirits (Mark 6:7), and they had been successful in casting out many demons and healing sick people (Mark 6:13). But in today's story the disciples just didn't have what it took to cast the evil spirit out of a boy and started arguing about it with the religious leaders who were there. Fortunately, Jesus arrived in time to help. Although there was a climate of doubt, Jesus acted on the bit of faith that the boy's father had and healed him.

Later, when Jesus was alone with his disciples, they discussed the failure. Jesus taught them that it takes more than past success to cast out demons—it takes a prayerful dependence on God.

Jesus got away from the crowds to take time alone to teach his disciples. He wanted to prepare them for his death even though they couldn't quite understand what he was talking about.

Look Back

Have you had a time when no matter how hard you tried, it seemed that evil won?

Have you had time alone with Jesus to ask him about it? If so, what did he say?

BreakThrough

Look Forward

Jesus wants to help us break through evil in our lives and in the lives of those we love. If you're presently up against evil that you can't break through, talk to Jesus about it. Write a prayer asking for help, then write what you sense God is saying to you about the situation.

Remember to keep praying for the miracles you asked for last week!

First Prize Goes to Last Place

Read: Mark 9:33-50

Jesus set out a difficult path to greatness in the Kingdom of God. Greatness in God's Kingdom is measured by taking last place, serving everyone else, welcoming children, giving a cup of cold water, living at peace. We don't have to be in the "in crowd" to be rewarded in the Kingdom of God. And the ultimate failure in God's Kingdom is causing a little one to lose faith.

Jesus makes it clear that we're probably going to have to give up some things that we are attached to if we want to start getting the benefits of Kingdom life here on earth. In order to enter into the life of the future here in the present, we have to give up anything that leads us into sin.

Look Back

It's interesting that Jesus didn't put down his disciples for striving for greatness. In fact, he told them how to succeed at being first in the Kingdom of God. Where have you tried to succeed in your life?

How do you think that might count for any success in the Kingdom of God?

BreakThrough

Look Forward

Where do you think God wants you to put your efforts for success now?

Who is God calling you to serve? (Maybe members of your family, co-workers, a special group of people God has placed on your heart?)

What is he asking you to do for them today? Write down your plan of action.

Remember: God wants to empower you with his Spirit to serve others, and he wants you to succeed in his Kingdom. He knows you need him!

Jesus Blesses Marriage and Children

Read: Mark 10:1-16

D ivorce was a reality in the world Jesus lived in, and the Pharisees wanted to trap Jesus into being either judgmental or lax. When questioned about it, Jesus said that divorce was a concession to "hard-hearted wickedness." Jesus wanted those around him to know that God had designed a better way, a way of joining two as one, unable to be separated: a life-long relationship between a man and a woman. That seemed to be as counter-cultural then as it is to most people in our modern day society. Life in the Kingdom is different than life in this present evil age.

Parents wanted Jesus to bless their children, so they brought them to him to have him place his hands on them. The disciples apparently thought Jesus was too busy for such an activity, but Jesus again pointed out that the Kingdom of God has different values than society. Jesus not only accepted children; he used them as role models!

Look Back

Jesus says in John 10:10, "the thief's (Satan's) purpose is to steal and kill and destroy. My purpose is to give life in all its fullness." Destroying marriages is one of Satan's most effective tools against society. Creating love-filled marriages is one of God's greatest gifts to us. When in your life have you experienced the pain of divorce?

BreakThrough

What marriages have you seen that model Kingdom living?

Look Forward

What children does God want you to bless?

Write down a plan of how you will do it.

Jesus Makes the Impossible Possible

Read: Mark 10:17-31

The rich man had been good as long as he could remember, but he knew he was missing something: eternal life. Jesus looked at him and loved him. Jesus' response was loving. He wasn't being mean. He wasn't trying to come up with something too difficult for the man so that he would just go away. He could see into the man's life and realized what it was that was keeping the man from receiving all that God had for him. Jesus made it clear that unless the man gave up all of his possessions and wealth, he would never have treasure in heaven. In fact, it was impossible for the rich to get into the Kingdom of God at all. The disciples wondered who could be saved, and Jesus replied that only God could make it possible.

Peter pointed out that he and the others (unlike the rich man) had left behind everything to follow Jesus. Jesus replied that the benefits of eternal life would begin now with belonging in a community-rich relationship with God and his people, even though those benefits would come side-by-side with persecutions. Eternal life would be fully experienced in the world to come. It seems that as a side note Jesus added that trying to be great (whether through accumulating or through giving up everything) was no guarantee of importance in God's Kingdom.

Look Back

Note that in this passage different words are used to express the same thing: get eternal life, have treasure in heaven, enter the Kingdom of God, be saved. Eternal life begins now, but we have

BreakThrough

to put up with the painful realities of the present (we call this the already-and-not-yet). Have you experienced any persecution from following Christ? If so, what happened?

What benefits would you say you've received already from following Jesus? In other words, how are you already experiencing eternal life?

Look Forward

"What should I do to get eternal life?" This is a question we each must ask. A similar question is, "How can I experience more of the Kingdom of God right now?" Choose one of these questions and ask God in prayer. Sit quietly and contemplate what God is saying to you, then write what you are sensing.

BreakThrough   ... of True Power

Week Five Introduction

Mark 11:24
"Listen to me! You can pray for anything, and if you believe, you will have it."

Throughout Mark we have seen the power of God's Kingdom breaking through in different ways. In Jesus there was and still is power to cast out demons (Mark 3:22), power to heal (Mark 5:30), and power to perform miracles (Mark 6:2).

Jesus' growing popularity, however, was creating increasing opposition by the powers that be. As he traveled to Jerusalem he knew his fate. His obedience to the Father would mean his betrayal and a gruesome death. All those traveling with him could feel the tension in the air as he set out. Mark 10:32 relates: "They were now on the way to Jerusalem, and Jesus was walking ahead of them. The disciples were filled with dread and the people following behind were overwhelmed with fear."

Although the crowds enthusiastically cheered Jesus' arrival in Jerusalem, his authority clashed with the authority of the religious leaders there. The story became somber and filled with conflict. Two paths were apparent—the way of the world and the way of God, the power of this world or the power that God offers.

As Jesus' fate was becoming clearer in the story, other fates were also being revealed. A withered fig tree and the story of a vineyard pointed to people who would reject their true king.

Earlier, Jesus had foretold his fate and called his disciples to follow him by giving their all. Jesus was now following through on the path he had spoken of, day-by-day and step-by-step walking out the Father's plan for him.

BreakThrough
... of True Power

Sometimes where we most need God's help is in living out His plan on a daily basis. Often the most difficult challenge to fulfill is not the large sacrifice or the spectacular risk that God puts before us, but the steady obedience of listening to him, seeking first his Kingdom and walking with him through the ups and downs of everyday life. This week's reading invites us to listen to his voice and follow his ways in a profound manner in our perplexing world.

BreakThrough

Jesus Heads to Jerusalem to Die

Read: Mark 10:32-52

Jesus was leaving his ministry in Galilee to go to Jerusalem. His disciples were convinced that he was the Messiah and were hoping he would overthrow the Romans. Though they were afraid of what might happen in Jerusalem, they didn't understand that Jesus knew he was going to be killed. In fact, James and John were hoping for the seats of honor next to him when he finally set up his "glorious Kingdom" (Mark 10:37). But Jesus hadn't changed his mind about the kind of king he would be, or the kind of Kingdom he would rule. He would give his life for others. In his Kingdom, servants would lead; the least would be first.

As if to illustrate his point, Jesus healed Bartimaeus. Blind beggars were looked down upon as among the "least" of society. Jesus took compassion on Bartimaeus and healed him in response to his cry. He allowed Bartimaeus to follow him on the way to Jerusalem.

By the time Jesus and his disciples had gone through Jericho, a great crowd had joined them. They were all journeying together to reach Jerusalem to celebrate the Passover according to custom. When Bartimaeus called out to Jesus, "Son of David," he was proclaiming to the crowd his belief that Jesus was the Messiah; for the first time publicly Jesus did not try to keep his identity quiet.

Look Back

Jesus' disciples were "filled with dread" as they headed with him toward Jerusalem.

Write below about a time when you were afraid of what was

ahead. How did God help you through that time?

Look Forward

Mark 10:32 says, "They were now on the way to Jerusalem, and Jesus was walking ahead of them." Where are you heading now? Write down where you think Jesus is leading you.

What difficulties might lie ahead of you?

Pray for the power of the Holy Spirit to serve wherever God leads you.

Jesus Promises Power in Prayer

Read: Mark 11:1-26

Jesus knew that Israel's Messiah would come victoriously into Jerusalem riding on a donkey's colt (Zechariah 9:9). The Galilean crowd following him also knew this and joyfully responded by praising Jesus from Psalm 118:25-26. This show of praise from the crowd acknowledged that they believed Jesus was the descendent of King David who would now come into power.

The next day Jesus asserted his authority by challenging temple worship using a public protest. He pointed out that the temple should be a place of prayer, not of conducting business. The religious leaders immediately recognized that he was their enemy. The new crowd of people he was attracting in Jerusalem responded enthusiastically.

Jesus gave a symbolic picture of Jerusalem's spiritual state by withering the fig tree. The tree had looked promising because of its many leaves, but Jesus cursed it because it was producing no fruit. This portrayed how Jesus was rejecting the temple system because of its lack of fruit. The temple would no longer be the place of prayer. Now anyone who prayed anywhere in faith would see God do miraculous things – if they had forgiven from their heart. In the Kingdom of God, the condition of the heart matters more than observing religious rites.

Look Back

1 Corinthians 6:19-20 teaches us that our bodies are now the temple of the Holy Spirit. How has your life changed as a result of Jesus cleansing your "temple" by identifying activities that were detrimental to your growth as a Christian? Explain.

BreakThrough

Have you allowed Jesus to make you into a "house (person) of prayer?" What things in your life are keeping you from praying? List any obstacles that come to mind.

Look Forward

Jesus tells us that we will receive what we ask for in prayer if we believe and if we forgive. What is God leading you to believe Him for in prayer? Who might you need to forgive first?

Is this a step you can take on your own, or do you need some help? If you need help, whom do you need to talk to in order to get the help you need?

Contact this person today, or as soon as possible. Remember to keep praying for miracles! (refer back to page 40)

BreakThrough

Jesus Announces New Leadership

Read: Mark 11:27-12:12

When asked where he got his authority, Jesus referred to John's baptism. John taught that his baptism was with water; the person who was coming would baptize with the Holy Spirit (see Mark 1:1-8). John had proclaimed that the Lord was coming – someone so great that John wasn't even worthy to be his slave. Jesus asked the religious leaders if they believed that John's baptism was indeed from God. If they admitted that John's baptism was from God, they would essentially be saying that Jesus was Lord. If they denied John's God-given authority, the crowd surrounding them might revolt. So the religious leaders didn't bother answering Jesus' question.

Jesus went on to tell a story that clearly put down those he was arguing with. The image of Jerusalem as a vineyard was used extensively in the Old Testament. Therefore, the audience would have known that Jesus was referring to Jerusalem as the vineyard and its leaders as the tenants. They also would have guessed that Jesus was referring to himself as the son sent as the father's last hope for the tenants's repentance. The son was murdered and his body thrown out. The owner of the vineyard killed the tenants and replaced them.

Jesus goes on to compare the stone the builders rejected to the son the tenants threw out. Just as the rejected stone became the most important stone in the building, so Jesus, the rejected son, would become the most important person in the new leadership of the God's people.

BreakThrough

Look Back

The Jewish leaders did not want to acknowledge Jesus' authority. They were in control, and they liked it that way. Jesus challenged their authority. Have you ever sensed Jesus challenging you to give up control of your life to him? How did you respond?

Have there been areas in your life that you have had difficulty in surrendering to Jesus? Did you resist him or allow him to take control and teach you a better way?

Look Forward

Jesus still challenges those who keep control of things and don't submit to him. He wants full authority over your life. Where in your life do you want to submit more fully to Jesus' kingship?

Write a prayer of submission to the Lord. He's willing to do awesome things in your life if you will allow him to.

BreakThrough

Jesus Answers Questions

Read: Mark 12:13-27

I n today's reading the Sadducees asked Jesus two difficult questions. If Jesus had been planning to overthrow the Roman government and set up his own earthly Kingdom, he would have answered the first question differently. His answer indicated that to belong to the Kingdom of God did not exempt anyone from being a responsible citizen to whatever earthly government they happened to live under. Obeying Caesar did not necessarily conflict with obeying God.

In response to the second question, Jesus pointed out that the Sadducees had made a serious error; they didn't know the Scriptures or the power of God. Their question made no sense. While he assured them that life continues after death, he pointed out that the nature of relationships in heaven was beyond their understanding.

Look Back

Do you have any questions that you've been asking God but don't seem to be getting any answers? Write down any questions you have about life, God, or Christianity that have never been answered for you.

BreakThrough

Look Forward

C.S. Lewis writes, "When I lay these questions before God I get no answer. But a rather special sort of 'no answer.' It is not the locked door. It is more like a silent, certainly not uncompassionate, gaze. As though He shook His head not in refusal but waiving the question. Like, 'Peace, child; you don't understand.'

"Can a mortal ask questions which God finds unanswerable? Quite easily, I should think. All nonsense questions are unanswerable. How many hours are there in a mile? Is yellow square or round? Probably half the questions we ask – half our great theological and metaphysical problems – are like that" (*A Grief Observed*, p. 87).

Let the Holy Spirit show you whether to keep asking the questions you wrote on the previous page, or whether they arise from a serious error: you don't know the Scriptures or the power of God. Cross out any questions you think are "nonsense questions." Ask God to help you understand his response to the questions you still have. Expect him to speak to you, and be patient as you seek his answers to the questions in your heart.

BreakThrough

Week Five
Day Five

Jesus Honors Those Who Give All to God

Read: Mark 12:28-44

In yesterday's reading, religious leaders asked Jesus trick questions. But today's question came from a sincere person whose heart desired to please God: What is the most important commandment? Interestingly, Jesus doesn't give him one commandment but two. Loving God is tied to loving others. Jesus wants us restored to relationship with God and relationship with one another.

Jesus taught that while "the Son of David" was a popular title for the Messiah, it was not an adequate title. David himself had referred to the Messiah as "Lord" in Psalm 110, so it must mean that the Messiah is superior to any earthly king. The Messiah's mission was much greater than ruling the nation of Israel.

Jesus then contrasted the attitude of the wealthy teachers of religious law with a poor widow. The former took from life all they could get; the widow gave all she had. Jesus taught that the teachers of the law would receive great punishment for their actions. The widow received his praise.

Look Back

What person or thing have you placed the most value on in your life?

Evaluate your giving. How have you used the resources that God has given you? How generous have you been?

BreakThrough

Write down a few thoughts about how you've used your money. What might you need to change or confess?

Look Forward

What portion of your income do you plan to give to God this year? (see 2 Corinthians 8:11-12; 9:6-9)

In what practical ways can you use your money to express your love for God and others? (see 1 John 3:16-18)

Ask God to continue to make you into a person willing to give all to him!

BreakThrough ... of the Future

Week Six Introduction

Mark 13:31
*"Heaven and earth will disappear, but my words will
remain forever."*

A s the story progressed, Jesus pointed to the future. He told
his followers of Jerusalem's pending fate. He spoke of the
end of the world. He pointed to the events engulfing him
that were immediately at hand. The pace of the drama picked up
speed as it began to reach its climax.

In the swirl of events one individual stood out. She seemed to
sense Jesus' needs and wanted to express her overflowing gratitude.
She poured her costly perfume on Jesus, filling the home where he
was being entertained with the fragrant evidence of her devotion.
No one understood her actions. They considered her stupid and
wasteful. They angrily berated her, but Jesus defended her.

Perhaps she sensed his impending death. Or maybe she per-
ceived the weight on his heart or the sadness in his eyes. Her sole
motivation was love for her Master. How would we have reacted
in this situation? Would our own hearts have been guided by an
overwhelming devotion to Christ, or by the earthly perspective
shared by the disciples? What is motivating our hearts today?

On his final evening with his disciples, Jesus gave them a tangi-
ble symbol to capture and convey the meaning of what was about
to take place. As they shared their last meal he gave them bread,
declaring, "Take it, for this is my body" (14:22). Then he passed
a cup of wine, announcing, "This is my blood, poured out for
many, sealing the covenant between God and his people. I solemnly
declare that I will not drink wine again until that day when I drink

it new in the Kingdom of God" (Mark 14:24-25).

This vivid sign explained the significance of what would soon take place. Jesus' death was for them and all people. God was making a new covenant, an unbreakable agreement. Now he would deal with us not on the basis of what we have done, but instead on the basis of what Christ has done for us. How wonderful and incredible! Through his death, Jesus explained, God was shaping a new people. We celebrate the same covenant every time we take the Lord's supper. We look to the past, recalling Jesus' blood shed for us. We share his grace personally and together in the present. And we look expectantly to the future when God's Kingdom will come in all its fullness.

Jesus Shares What Lies Ahead

Read: Mark 13:1-23

As Jesus was leaving the temple, he predicted that it would be destroyed. Later, when he was alone with a small group of his disciples, he answered their questions about when this would happen and how they would know it was coming. He told them that they could expect wars and famines and persecutions. On the positive side, news about him would have reached to those outside of Israel, and the Holy Spirit would give them the words to say whenever they needed to defend themselves in court. But the temple would be destroyed during a time of incredible horrors, and false Messiahs would try to deceive them. They needed to watch out!

Look Back

What have you wanted to know about the future?

What have you done to prepare for life beyond this world?

BreakThrough

Look Forward

In this passage Jesus made it clear to his disciples that difficult times were coming. But in verse 7 He told them not to panic. And in verse 13 he said, "Those who endure to the end will be saved." If you encountered severe persecution because of your allegiance to Jesus, how strong do you think your faith would be?

Pray for those around the world who are currently suffering arrests, persecution, and betrayal because of their faith in Jesus, and all who are in desperate conditions because of famines and war.

Jesus Warns His Disciples to Keep Watch

Read: Mark 13:24-37

J esus was still talking to four of his disciples about when the
temple would be destroyed. But he had some good news to
share about it. After the horrible days ended, the powers of
heaven would be shaken in such a way that the Son of Man would
rule with great power and glory. He would gather people from the
farthest ends of the earth—not just Israel! Jesus assured them that
the Temple would be destroyed during their generation, and even
heaven and earth would eventually disappear, but his words would
remain forever.

Jesus then reminded his disciples that since they could not
know when these things would take place, they needed to stay on
guard. Just as employees need to work while the owner is gone, so
Jesus' disciples would have to work until Jesus returned. Only the
Father knows when that day will come.

Look Back

What types of things have you been asked to do in the past
without supervision?

Did you fulfill your responsibilities? What were the conse-
quences/results?

BreakThrough

Look Forward

What work are you to be doing as you wait for Jesus' return?

How diligent are you in doing this work?

Write a prayer asking God to show you what more He has for you to do. Listen for his response. Pray for perseverance to do the work God has for you until He takes you to be with him.

BreakThrough

Jesus Is Anointed for His Burial

Read: Mark 14:1-11

The religious leaders got serious about putting Jesus to death after the embarrassing debates and heated conflict about the temple (Mark 11:15-13:2). They hoped to accomplish it before the Passover.

While Jesus was eating supper, a woman came and poured costly perfume on his head. The men at the table considered it a great waste, but Jesus cherished the act as a preparation for his burial. Even though he sensed the nearness of his death, he had confidence that the Good News would be preached throughout the world and that this woman's story would be remembered. He honored her for doing what she could with what she had.

Judas chose not to accept the life Jesus offered, where the least of society became the most honored, and he arranged to hand Jesus over to those seeking to kill him.

Look Back

Sometimes we want to serve Jesus extravagantly like this woman, with hearts full of thankfulness. Write about a personal experience with this type of worship (or an example of someone else's).

Take time to write down anything that comes to mind that you can thank God for to help you develop a grateful heart that overflows in worship.

BreakThrough

Look Forward

How can you best express your love for Jesus today?

What "expensive perfume" can you pour out? Jesus will honor you for it!

BreakThrough

Jesus Shares Passover with Disciples

Read: Mark 14:12-25

The sun had set; the first day of the Festival of Unleavened Bread had begun (Jews consider sunset to sunset a day). The Passover lambs would be sacrificed before the sun set again. Jesus knew his time was running short and ordered the preparations for the Passover meal that evening. There was a somber atmosphere: the disciples were distressed by Jesus' comments that he must die and that one of them would betray him. They heard Jesus' hard words spoken against that one. They shared together the broken bread that represented Jesus' broken body and the wine representing his blood. They heard his solemn declaration that he would not drink wine again until he drank it new in the Kingdom of God.

Look Back

Jesus knew he was facing certain death, but he also knew he had a future beyond death. How have people in your family and those close to you faced death?

What impact has that had on your view of life and death?

BreakThrough

Look Forward

What (if anything) do you fear about dying?

What (if anything) do you look forward to?

Share with God in prayer about what you've written.

BreakThrough

Jesus Has Good News to Share

Read: Mark 1:1-20

After eating the Passover meal, Jesus and his disciples left Jerusalem and walked to the Mount of Olives singing hymns, probably from Psalms 115-118, as part of the ritual of the Passover meal. Jesus warned his disciples that they would all desert him. God would strike him and they would all be scattered. He tried to encourage them with the thought that he would rise from the dead and be with them again in Galilee – their home – where they had seen so many wonderful miracles. Peter, overly confident, declared that he would never desert Jesus. But Jesus knew better and predicted that Peter would in fact deny him 3 times before the rooster crowed the next morning.

As we have seen him do earlier in the Gospel of Mark, Jesus again went off to pray. He knew he needed strength to go through the ordeal that was facing him, and he ran to his Father for help. How he longed for the support of his friends in this difficult hour, but they were too sleepy. They did not comprehend the imminence of his death. Through prayer Jesus gained the strength he needed from his Father and was ready to face his betrayer.

Look Back

Jesus wanted the support of his friends, but they didn't have what it took to stay awake. Write about when you have felt deserted in a time of need or when you have felt that others didn't really understand the pressure you were facing in a situation.

BreakThrough

Write about how God provided for you during that time. Then, thank him. If you aren't sure how God provided for you, ask him to show you how he was faithful to you even when others were not.

Look Forward

Where in your life do you need God's strength?

What songs can you sing to put your heart in the right place? (Jesus sang songs from the Psalms).

Write a prayer asking God for whatever you need right now.

Break**Through**

Week Seven Introduction

Mark 15:39

"When the Roman officer who stood facing him saw how he had died, he exclaimed, 'Truly, this was the Son of God!' "

D o not be surprised. You are looking for Jesus, the Nazarene, who was crucified. He isn't here! He has been raised from the dead!" (Mark 16:6).

As our story moved forward, the forces of the world converged to put Jesus to death. In crucifying the Son of God, earthly power in all forms— politicians, religious leaders, soldiers, and crowds—united to destroy him. He was bludgeoned, mocked, and spit on. A crown of thorns was thrust on his head as his tormentors shouted, "Hail, King of the Jews" (Mark 15:18). Jesus suffered indescribable physical pain. He experienced the sting of betrayal and the loneliness of desertion. Perhaps his greatest anguish was his separation from his Heavenly Father as the weight of the world's sin fell upon him. As he hung dying, his kingship was mocked by the placard nailed to the cross: "The King of the Jews" (15:26). But beneath the surface of events, beneath what the human eye could see, cataclysmic events were taking place. The foundations of the universe were being shaken. The power of Satan was being broken. What looked like the ultimate defeat of God's Kingdom was actually its ultimate victory.

As Jesus was dying, the Jerusalem temple stood across town. Its innermost sanctum was called the "holy of holies." This inmost part of the temple represented the inapproachable presence of God. The only person who could enter it was the high priest, and he only did this once a year to offer a sacrifice of atonement for the sins of God's people. He would enter the "holy of holies" with a rope tied about his ankle so that if he died there, he could be pulled back out. The holy of holies was separated from the "most holy place" by a thick multi-layered curtain. As Jesus breathed his last breath, Mark tells us that the "curtain in the temple was torn in two, from top to bottom" (Mark 15:38).

The barrier of sin had been destroyed. Now we all can freely access the presence, mercy, and grace of God because of all that Jesus did for us!

But Jesus' death was not the end of the story. Thank God! He then rose from the dead! Jesus' followers never really understood or believed what he told them about his approaching death. They were shocked when he was arrested, beaten, and crucified. They were even more confused when he rose from the dead. Can you image the emotions of joy and bewilderment when some of them received this angelic message at his tomb: "Do not be so surprised. You are looking for Jesus, the Nazarene, who was crucified. He isn't here! He has been raised from the dead!" (16:6).

The Gospel of Mark begins with the words, "The beginning of the gospel about Jesus Christ, the Son of God" (1:1, NIV). It's as if Mark was saying, "The story I am about to tell you is just the beginning of the good news of Jesus." The good news continues today as the living Christ continues his work through us. With his power and presence, we are invited to continue his ministry. Together with him and one another, we are invited to experience and extend his Kingdom – his truth, his love, and his power.

BreakThrough

Jesus Chooses Obedience

Read: Mark 14:43-72

Jesus had predicted that he would be betrayed, ridiculed, and killed (see Mark 10:33-34; 14:27-31). Now the time had come for these prophecies to be fulfilled. Each person had a choice of response. Judas chose to betray. Other disciples chose to flee. Witnesses chose to lie. The religious leaders and guards chose to capture Jesus, condemn him for blasphemy, and ridicule him rather than believing him. Peter chose to deny him.

And what did Jesus choose? He chose to follow the course his Father had set for him. He did not resist. He knew the time had come for him to die. After months of secrecy, he revealed himself as the Messiah, the Son of Man, the one who is in a place of authority at God's right hand.

Look Back

What choices have you made in response to Christ's work in your life as you have been reading the Gospel of Mark?

Glance through the last six weeks and prayerfully consider how God has spoken to you and how you have responded to him. Write your thoughts down.

BreakThrough

Look Forward

Psalm 37:5 says, "Commit everything you do to the Lord. Trust him, and he will help you." Even in our day-to-day routines, we face decisions of whether we will spend our time on ourselves or in worship to God. What circumstances and decisions are you facing?

What choices do you feel the Lord is leading you to make?

Write a prayer of commitment to the Lord (and he will help you).

BreakThrough

Jesus Is the King of the Jews

Read: Mark 15:1-20

Jesus continued to choose to follow through with what his Father had asked him to do. Pilate gave him the opportunity to defend himself against all the charges brought against him. But to Pilate's surprise, Jesus accepted the title of King of the Jews and made no further statements.

Pilate wondered if the crowd gathered would like him to release "the King of the Jews." But the crowd had no desire to free a man who wasn't willing to stand up in defense against the Romans. They wanted Barabbas, who had taken part in an insurrection. The Romans might as well crucify Jesus.

Jesus was flogged and sent on his way to crucifixion. To humiliate him as much as possible, the soldiers mocked Jesus by dressing him in "royal" clothes and crown, beat him, spit on him, and bowed before him. The story unfolded just as Jesus had foretold.

Look Back

In this passage we read of the horrible treatment Jesus endured as part of his sacrifice for us. Isaiah prophesied, "It was our (my) weaknesses he carried; it was our (my) sorrows that weighed him down ... But he was wounded and crushed for our (my) sins. He was beaten that we (I) might have peace. He was whipped, and we were (I was) healed!" (Isaiah 53:4-5).

Meditate on this passage from Isaiah. Think of the sacrifice Jesus made for you. Let the reality of God's deep love for you penetrate your heart and mind. "For God so loved the world (me)

BreakThrough

that he gave his only Son, so that whoever believes in him (I) will not perish but have eternal life" (John 3:16).

Write down some of your thoughts about God's amazing love for you.

Look Forward

Write a prayer expressing your response to God's great love for you.

Jesus Dies Amidst Ridicule

Read: Mark 15:21-39

The final blow was delivered. Jesus was nailed to the cross, abandoned by his disciples, surrounded by ridicule. Even the light of day disappeared, and his Father forsook him. He cried out in pain and died.

But behind all the horror and pain was a glimmer of hope. Centuries earlier this treatment had been prophesied in Psalm 22, and that psalm ended in victory and praise. As Jesus died, the curtain in the temple was torn from top to bottom, symbolizing that the role of the temple was over: Jesus was opening a new way of approaching God.

In the moment that seemed to indicate Jesus' total failure, a Roman officer on the scene unexpectedly proclaimed his victory: "Truly, this was the Son of God!"

Look Back

Jesus died for us, and his death ended in great victory over the power of sin. Galatians 3:13 states, "But Christ has rescued us from the curse pronounced by the law. When he was hung on the cross, he took upon himself the curse for our wrongdoing. For it is written in the Scriptures, 'Cursed is everyone who is hung on a tree.'"

We have all experienced the curse of wrongdoing because we have experienced negative consequences either from our own sins or from someone else's sin. This may be from an individual's sin, or the sins of society (such as prejudice).

BreakThrough

What sins did Jesus die to set you free from? What curse did Jesus take on himself for you?

What personal victories have you experienced because Jesus died for you and defeated the power of sin?

Look Forward

"So just as sin ruled over all people and brought them to death, now God's wonderful kindness rules instead, giving us right standing with God and resulting in eternal life through Jesus Christ our Lord" (Romans 5:21). Where do you need victory over evil? Or who is someone dear to you that is in need of freedom from sin?

Write a prayer of faith that the victory Christ won would be accomplished in this area: that there would be a breakthrough of the Kingdom of God!

Jesus' Friends Attend to His body

Read: Mark 15:40-16:8

Jesus was dead. Some women who had been followers of Jesus watched from a distance and saw him die. Although criminals who were crucified were not usually allowed a proper burial, Joseph of Arimathea gathered courage to ask permission to bury Jesus in his own tomb. So Jesus was quickly buried before sunset when the Sabbath began.

As soon as the sun had set the next day, the Sabbath ended and business was allowed again. The women bought spices to put on Jesus' body. As soon as it was light the next morning, the women went to the tomb to finish the proper burial procedure.

But instead of finding a stiff body, they found an angel that frightened them stiff. Although the angel gave the women a message of hope to deliver, they were so frightened they couldn't even talk.

Look Back

Joseph of Arimathea and the women did what they could for Jesus even when it seemed that he had failed them. Write about a time in your life when God took a bad situation and turned it around for you?

BreakThrough

Write a prayer of thanks to God for being with you in difficult circumstances (even if you haven't seen anything good come of it yet).

Look Forward

The angel gave the women a message to share: "Jesus is alive and is going ahead of you. You will see him in the places you feel at home at" (Mark 16:6-7). You have been given the same message to give to your friends. What's your response to this message to share?

Write a prayer to God about it.

Jesus Has Good News to Share

Read: Mark 16:9-20

Jesus was alive! Mary Magdalene saw him, and two men leaving Jerusalem saw him, but no one would believe them. When he later appeared to his disciples, Jesus rebuked them for their unbelief.

But Jesus had great news to share with them! He wanted the good news preached everywhere so everyone could believe in him and be saved. He would continue to deliver and heal those who came to him.

Jesus left his disciples and returned to the place of honor with God in heaven. But he didn't abandon them, and he hasn't abandoned us. He has given us his Holy Spirit to be in us, empowering us to continue his ministry. Just as he did two thousand years ago, he is still working with us, confirming what is preached in his name by many miraculous signs!

Look Back

Who have been the most influential people helping you grow in your Christian faith?

What have they said and done to help you the most?

BreakThrough

Look Forward

How do you want God to use you to spread the good news of his truth, love, and power?

Write a prayer asking the Holy Spirit to empower you to do all he asks of you!

Bibliography

Several books were very helpful as we prepared these materials. If you want to explore Jesus' message of the Kingdom of God or the Gospel of Mark, we highly recommend the following scholarly resources:

France, R.T. <u>The People's Bible Commentary</u>. Mark. Oxford: The Bible Reading Fellowship, 1996.

France, R.T. <u>The New International Greek Testament Commentary</u>. Grand Rapids, MI: Eerdmans Publishing Co., 2002.

France, R.T. <u>Divine Government: God's Kinship in the Gospel of Mark</u>. Vancouver, British Columbia: Regent College Publishing, 2003.

Ladd, George Eldon. <u>The Gospel of the Kingdom</u>. Grand Rapids, MI: Eerdmans Publishing Co., 1959.

Morphew, Derek. <u>Breakthrough: Discovering the Kingdom</u>. Cape Town, South Africa: Vineyard International Publishing, 1991.

Wright, N.T. <u>The Challenge of Jesus: Rediscovering Who Jesus Was and Is</u>. Downers Grove, IL: InterVarsity Press, 1999.

BreakThrough

BreakThrough

Personal notes

Personal notes **Break**Through

God's Relentless Pursuit: Discovering His Heart for Humanity
by Phil Strout
retail price: $10.95

Have you ever considered that instead of us chasing God, He is actually the One chasing us? In his book, author Phil Strout explores God's mission on earth and how His people join in His mission: to draw people into relationship with Him. Many common ideas and notions regarding our role in pursuing God are challenged as we discover the truth about what God is doing in and around us, both across the street and across the oceans.

Sample chapters and book are available for purchase at: www.ampelonpublishing.com

Passionate Pursuit: Discovering the Heart of Christ
by Jason Chatraw
retail price: $8.95

Do you want to experience a greater intimacy in the time you spend with God? If so, the devotional *Passionate Pursuit* helps set you on the right path. We must know that our relationship with God is a journey, not a quick trip. And being equipped for the journey will make it more fun and exciting.

Sample chapters and book are available for purchase at: www.ampelonpublishing.com

For more small group resources and devotionals, visit our website at: www.ampelonpublishing.com